Blessed James Alberione

Media Apostle

Anne Eileen Heffernan, FSP

Illustrated by Charlie Craig

BOOKS & MEDIA
Boston

Library of Congress Cataloging-in-Publication Data

Heffernan, Eileen.
Blessed James Alberione : media apostle / Anne Eileen Heffernan, FSP ; illustrated by Charlie Craig.
pages cm. -- (Encounter the saints series)
ISBN-13: 978-0-8198-1213-1
ISBN-10: 0-8198-1213-7
1. Alberione, James, 1884-1971. 2. Catholic Church--Italy--Clergy--Biography. 3. Mass media in religion. I. Title.
BX4705.A429H44 2013
271′.79--dc23
[B]

2013005202

Cover art/illustrated by Charlie Craig

Published by Pauline Books & Media, 50 Saint Pauls Avenue, Boston, MA 02130-3491

Printed in U.S.A.

BJAM VSAUSAPEOILL8-5J13-07022 1213-7

www.pauline.org

Pauline Books & Media is the publishing house of the Daughters of St. Paul, an international congregation of women religious serving the Church with the communications media.

1 2 3 4 5 6 7 8 9 17 16 15 14 13

Dedicated to the young future members
of the Pauline Family

Encounter the Saints Series

Blesseds Jacinta and Francisco Marto
Shepherds of Fatima

Blessed John Paul II
The People's Pope

Blessed Pier Giorgio Frassati
Journey to the Summit

Blessed Teresa of Calcutta
Missionary of Charity

Journeys with Mary
Apparitions of Our Lady

Saint Anthony of Padua
Fire and Light

Saint Bakhita of Sudan
Forever Free

Saint Bernadette Soubirous
And Our Lady of Lourdes

Saint Catherine Labouré
And Our Lady of the Miraculous Medal

Saint Clare of Assisi
A Light for the World

Saint Damien of Molokai
Hero of Hawaii

Saint Edith Stein
Blessed by the Cross

Saint Elizabeth Ann Seton
Daughter of America

Saint Faustina Kowalska
Messenger of Mercy

Saint Frances Xavier Cabrini
Cecchina's Dream

Saint Francis of Assisi
Gentle Revolutionary

Saint Gianna Beretta Molla
The Gift of Life

Saint Ignatius of Loyola
For the Greater Glory of God

Saint Isaac Jogues
With Burning Heart

Saint Joan of Arc
God's Soldier

Saint John Vianney
A Priest for All People

Saint Juan Diego
And Our Lady of Guadalupe

Saint Katharine Drexel
The Total Gift

Saint Martin de Porres
Humble Healer

Saint Maximilian Kolbe
Mary's Knight

Saint Paul
The Thirteenth Apostle

Saint Pio of Pietrelcina
Rich in Love

Saint Teresa of Avila
Joyful in the Lord

Saint Thérèse of Lisieux
The Way of Love

For other children's titles on the saints, visit our Web site: www.pauline.org.

Contents

1
Farm Boy

It was an early April afternoon in northern Italy, and the air was cool. A middle-aged farmer knocked briskly on the door of his pastor's house.

"Is Father in?" he asked the housekeeper as she opened the door. "I'm Michael Alberione (Al- BARE-ee-OH-nay) from New Ponds Farm."

"Yes, indeed, I'm here," said the priest, coming up behind the housekeeper. "Come in, Michael, come in." He led Mr. Alberione into his parlor. As they sat down, he asked, "Is your family well?"

"Yes, Father," replied the farmer. "Except for our new son, who was born this morning. He's small and very thin. I'm afraid he may not live, and Teresa—my wife—is worried, too. We wondered if we could have him baptized tomorrow."

"I don't see why not," replied the priest. "Are the godparents nearby?"

"The godmother lives nearby. She's Teresa's sister and is at the house now, to help her. But the godfather, my brother James, lives farther away, and it feels like a storm is coming."

In farming country in 1884 it was hard to send messages quickly. There were no cars yet, and no telephones.

"I could substitute for your brother," offered the priest kindly.

"Thank you very much, Father," replied the farmer. "What time shall we bring our little James?"

"Ten o'clock in the morning will be fine," Father said.

After thanking the priest again, Michael Alberione returned to the farm he was renting.

He and Teresa, with their three sons, had moved to New Ponds Farm only last November. Yet already they felt that this was not the place for them.

The owner of the farm lived far away. He had rented a large room and the stable to the Alberione family. The Alberiones lived in the large room. At night the boys went to the stable to sleep.

Michael Alberione did not find it hard to live in one room and a stable. He had always been poor. What bothered him was the farmland. Even though there were two ponds, the ground was dry and hard. It was clay soil. The neighbors had told Mr. Alberione that his harvests would be poor. He would get very little profit to share with the farm's owner.

Many evenings Michael had told Teresa, "We need to find land that's better for farming. We're going to have to move our family again."

Baby James was baptized the next morning in the Church of Saint Lawrence. His father and Aunt Anna, his godmother, brought him home. They were happy that he had not caught cold. Anna placed him in his mother's arms. Teresa rejoiced that her youngest son was now a child of God, like his brothers.

At noon the family had a simple meal of celebration in their one large room. James lay in the cradle that each of his brothers had used before him. Papa Michael looked with pride at his new son and the three older boys. Juvenal (JOO-vuh-nuhl) was eight; John, five; and Francis, almost three. Smiling at his wife, Michael said, "We have four sons. Someday they'll be able to help with the farm work."

"Hurry, James, we need your light," called Mamma Teresa after supper one autumn evening. It was already dark, but James's parents and brothers were going out to the field to finish the autumn planting. James was no longer a baby. He was old enough to hold the lantern, so the others could see what they were doing. Small for his age, James struggled to keep up with everyone else as they walked toward the field.

One of his brothers joked, "James, that lantern is almost as big as you are!" The other boys laughed, too. James concentrated on keeping up.

When they reached the field, it was easier. Now everyone moved slowly, spread out in a row. James simply had to walk ahead, holding the lantern. His parents and brothers hoed the earth to cover the seed they had planted earlier in the day. The soil was not hard to hoe. The family had moved to a different farm, where the ground was better for growing crops.

James was glad to have his very own job. But he was tired, too. He couldn't see beyond the bright light of the lantern. He tried not to stumble as he moved ahead.

"James, give us light!" his mother called. Her little son was zigzagging from right to left and back again. He was falling asleep on his feet!

2

"THAT'S WHO I WANT TO BE!"

"James, keep an eye on your baby brother," said Mamma Teresa one morning. James was five now. Whenever his mother was busy, it was his job to rock the cradle of baby Thomas. This kept Thomas from crying. Mamma Teresa had brought the wooden cradle into the stable. As she left to take care of her household tasks, James began to rock the cradle gently. One of the cows had been kept inside that day. It watched the cradle-rocking with mild interest.

I'd really like to go outside, James thought. He knew it was too chilly to take the baby out unless he bundled him up. But it was not too cold to go outside himself. How could he get out and still take care of Thomas?

I know! James thought. *I'll put a rope out the window!* He took a coil of rope from the peg where it hung and tied one end to the cradle. He opened the window slightly and dropped the other end outside. He went out the door, pulled on the rope, and let it go, so

Suddenly there was a loud crash, followed by the cries of a frightened and angry baby.

the cradle would rock. This was a little more work than rocking the cradle by hand but he was happy to be out in the fresh air. He kept it up—pulling and letting go, pulling and letting go. Suddenly there was a loud crash, followed by the cries of a frightened and angry baby.

James and his mother arrived in the stable at the same moment. The five-year-old had been pulling too hard. The cradle had rocked so much that it had moved right behind the cow and turned over. Thomas lay on the floor near the cow, screaming.

Mamma Teresa rescued her little one. She held the wailing baby under one arm and with her free hand helped James turn the cradle right-side up. Together they pulled it away from the dangerous hooves of the cow. James untied the rope. He felt tears coming to his eyes.

"You know you shouldn't have done that," said Mamma Teresa, trying not to sound upset.

James nodded. Thomas continued to bawl.

"I won't do it again," said James.

Mamma Teresa managed to smile. "I know you won't," she said. She knew how serious James was about everything. He would remember this lesson.

James was beginning to learn about the world around him.

He liked to walk with his mother to a nearby town where there was a shrine to Mary, the Mother of Jesus. It was called Our Lady of the Flowers, and was a very special place for Mamma Teresa. At that shrine, she had placed each of her children under Mary's protection.

Two miles from the farm in another direction was the church of Saint Martin. Each Sunday the Alberione family walked to Saint Martin's to attend Mass. James liked the priest, Father John Montersino (MON-tare-SEE-noh), who was very kind. Near the church was the school that James's brother Francis attended.

When James was six, he began school himself. Right away, he liked his teacher, Miss Cardona. He liked school, too. He worked hard, learning how to read and write Italian. When he came home in the late afternoon, he would spend some time with Mamma Teresa, telling her what he had learned during the day. This was their special time together.

One day Miss Cardona asked a question that her pupils had to answer one by one: "What would you like to be when you grow up?"

The question took everyone by surprise. There was a moment of silence.

James wondered, *Who do I want to be like?* He thought about his father, who worked so hard in the fields. But he didn't think he wanted to work on the farm all his life.

Maybe Uncle James, he thought. *After all, he's my godfather*. But a businessman's life didn't seem very exciting to him.

Suddenly James pictured in his mind a tall man dressed in black. It was Father John, the kind pastor of Saint Martin's, who was always eager to listen to the people of the parish and help them.

He imagined how he himself would look all dressed in black. *That's it!* he thought. *That's who I want to be! I want to be Father Alberione!*

Miss Cardona had already called on one of her pupils. Now she fixed her gaze on James.

"What do you want to be, James Alberione?"

"I want to be a priest," he said clearly.

A murmur of surprise rippled through the classroom. "Can a farm boy become a priest?" one of James's friends asked in wonder.

"Quiet, children," said Miss Cardona. "That's a very worthwhile goal, James." She called on another boy, asking again, "And what do you want to be?"

James tried to pay attention to the others, but he couldn't. A wonderful thing had just happened to him. He knew he wanted to be a priest! He could hardly wait to tell his mother. How happy she would be!

Everybody in the family would be happy—wouldn't they?

3

"MARY WILL HELP ME"

That same afternoon James told his mother that he wanted to be a priest. She looked surprised and pleased. At supper, he was bursting to tell everyone else. His eyes were sparkling and he squirmed with excitement.

"James, what are you so excited about?" asked John.

"I decided today . . . I'm going to be a priest!" James exclaimed.

His brothers all started talking at once.

"A what?"

"How can *you* be a priest?"

"*Why* do you want to be a priest?"

James tried to explain to his brothers why he wanted to be a priest, but he couldn't find the right words. The reason wasn't clear to him yet. He simply knew that he *had* to be a priest.

Mamma Teresa kept quiet.

Papa Michael cleared his throat. "We've never had a priest in our family," he said.

"Then I'll be the first one!" replied James. Now he was even more excited.

But his father didn't look happy, and everyone else became quiet.

James was surprised. Papa Michael was a good Catholic. He was strict, but he took good care of his children. He went to church every Sunday. James had thought Papa Michael would be happy if one of his sons became a priest.

Michael Alberione began eating again, and the older boys started talking about other things.

James looked at his mother. Couldn't she say something? But Mamma Teresa only gave him a serious look and a slight shake of her head. That meant: *This isn't the time to talk about it*.

That night, when James curled up on the straw in the hayloft near his brothers, he felt confused. He had this wonderful plan, but nobody seemed to care, except his mother. And even she didn't want him to talk about it. As he lay there he wondered, *Why would Papa not be happy? Is it because he hoped I would help on the farm?* After he had stayed awake a long time worrying, he prayed silently to Mary. James always turned to the

Blessed Mother in all his needs. *She will help me,* he thought. *I know she will.*

James had been going to school for three years. By now, he was old enough to sometimes go alone to pray at the shrine of Our Lady of the Flowers. The chapel was some distance from the farm, but he was used to walking.

One day he went into the shrine, knelt down, and told Mary he was worried about how he was doing in school. He promised her that if he were promoted to the next grade, he would light a candle at the shrine. After praying, he hurried home to help with the farm work.

A few days later, he came in happily as Mamma Teresa was preparing supper. "Mamma, I was promoted!" he announced. "And I was first in the class," he added.

Mamma Teresa looked pleased. "Your good grades show that you worked hard," she said. Then she continued preparing supper. James wanted to tell her about his promise to Mary, but he didn't. The candle would cost money James didn't have.

A few days later, he cleared his conscience and told her the rest of the story.

"Mamma, before I took my exams I was worried, so I went to pray at the shrine of Our Lady."

His mother stopped working and looked at him. "You do that often," she said. "So why are you telling me this now?"

Then she became very serious. "James, did you promise to light a candle?"

James blushed and nodded.

"And you waited all this time to tell me?"

James looked at the floor and squirmed.

"Be very slow to promise, my son," said Mamma Teresa. "But once you've made a promise, be sure to keep your promise generously. Go, now, and don't light just a *little* candle."

She gave him a coin to cover the cost of a large candle. Joyfully James ran off to keep his promise.

By the time James turned ten, he had received the sacraments of Penance and Confirmation, which children received around the age of seven in those days. He had also made his First Communion, even though eight or nine was usually considered too early. Father John had believed James was ready. Lately, Father John had even given James some pamphlets about the missions. *I think I'd like to be a missionary priest,* James thought.

But would he become a priest at all? He was worried. His brothers had stopped going to school after third grade so they could help on the farm. James wanted to go much further. Otherwise, he wouldn't be able to enter the seminary, where boys studied to become priests. In James's time, boys could enter the seminary in sixth grade. They could begin to study subjects that would prepare them for the special studies men do in order to become priests.

I can't talk to Papa about it, James thought. *Every time I try, he pretends not to hear me.*

Mamma Teresa wasn't much help either. She just kept saying, "We'll see."

One day when his mother said, "We'll see," James blurted out, "Papa doesn't understand!"

"Don't talk like that," Mamma Teresa answered. "Your father could just as rightly say, '*James* doesn't understand.'"

What's there to understand? James wondered. *I'm supposed to become a priest.*

Mamma Teresa went on to explain. "When we moved to this farm," she said, "it was like a dream come true. Your father wants to save up so we can *buy* this farm. Your brothers have stopped attending school and are already helping with the farm work. When they're older we won't have to hire anyone else anymore. We can save up to buy the farm. But if the money we save has to be used to put you through the seminary, we can't buy the farm. So you see what a problem we have."

James stared at her. Was his dream going to die here and now? But then Mamma Teresa smiled and added, "I've always prayed that one of my sons would become a priest. If God has given you this vocation, we must pray and trust that the Lord will find a way for you to go to the seminary."

James nodded. He understood now that his mother was trying to do what was best for the whole family. He tried to smile. "I guess you're right," he said.

But how could his dream come true?

4

SURPRISES

It was a Sunday, and the family was having dinner.

Papa Michael cleared his throat. Everybody quieted down and looked at him. James wondered what was going on.

"A few days ago," Papa told the boys, "your mother and I asked Father John for advice. He suggested we try to put James through the seminary."

James wanted to shout for joy, but he only grinned. His mother smiled gently, with tears in her eyes. The expressions on the faces of the older boys were mixed. Thomas, who was only five, looked bewildered. "What's a seminary?" he asked, but nobody paid attention to him.

At last, James said, "Thank you, Papa and Mamma."

"You'll have some more years of school before entering the seminary," Papa added. "Meanwhile, help on the farm when you can, while we try to save enough money."

James thanked his parents again. His dream was going to come true after all! *I have to thank Father John,* he thought. *And thank you especially, Jesus!*

James continued school. Every day when he returned home, he would find a rake or hoe waiting for him in the field where his brothers were working. He would help on the farm until supper.

Now that James's dream seemed to be coming true, his brothers often teased him:

"Hey, priest, what took you so long?"

"Reverend Father, can you bring me a cup of water?"

"Watch it, priest, you slipped up here!"

The summer after fourth grade James studied hard every chance he got. He wanted to pass an exam that would allow him to skip fifth grade and enter the local secondary school, which started with sixth grade. Sometimes he saw Thomas watching him. One day the younger boy blurted out, "Why do you want to study all the time?"

James smiled. "Because I want to be a priest," he said.

At the end of the summer, James passed the special exam and then began secondary school.

It turned out to be a hard year. The following spring, he passed, but complained to Mamma Teresa, "My marks aren't as good as they used to be."

"It's only normal," his mother told him. "You skipped a grade. Everything is bound to be harder."

Then James said what was really on his mind. "Mamma, can't I enter the seminary this fall for seventh grade and continue school there?"

"We'll see," his mother replied. Then she changed the subject.

That night, however, when the boys had gone to the stable to sleep, Mamma Teresa said to her husband, "I think it's time for James to enter the seminary."

"He can continue going to school in town for now," Papa Michael replied. "It's so convenient—just a couple of miles away."

"But it's not the same," responded Mamma Teresa. "The secondary school here is a whole different atmosphere. He needs to be in a place that will help him prepare to be a priest. Father John can arrange for him to enter the seminary nearby."

Michael Alberione hesitated, and then replied, "I'm not sure we can afford it. Except for vacations, James would have to live at the seminary and that can be expensive. Otherwise he'd spend all his time walking back and forth and wouldn't be able to study." After Papa Michael thought for a few moments, he sighed and added, "I'll see if it's possible."

Amazingly enough, it happened! That autumn, twelve-year-old James entered seventh grade at the seminary. Although it was hard to leave his parents and brothers, James was where he needed to be so that his dream to become a priest could happen.

He was so happy! He liked the teachers, the school subjects, and praying together with the other boys. Living at the seminary was a little different than being home. For one thing, he no longer slept in the hayloft. Everyone ate in a large dining room called a refectory with food prepared by cooks. But James thought the best part was the chapel. He enjoyed praying silently near the tabernacle of the chapel, where Jesus was present in the Blessed Sacrament. He prayed much and still managed to get his homework done.

He was glad they were able to go to Mass every day. *A few years from now,* James thought, *I'll be celebrating Mass every day myself.*

Most of the other boys were from town, and their families were better off than James's family. Some of the town boys weren't very friendly at first, but as time went on they began to like this quiet boy from the farm.

In general, the priests at the seminary also liked James. The only fault they found in him was his habit of slipping away from the group of boys when they all went for a Sunday afternoon walk.

"Where do you go?" one of the priests asked James once.

"Both my parents have relatives here," the boy explained. "I like to drop in on them."

It was a busy life—whether at the seminary or on the farm during vacation. At home, he now had his own room with a cot and desk. A storage area on the second floor had been cleared out, so he would have a place to study when he wasn't helping with the farm work. Three happy years passed by, and fifteen-year-old James expected his fourth year at the seminary to be the same. But that year would be very different.

5

SLIPPERY SLOPE

"Here, James. This is something else you should know about."

It was a magazine, opened to a particular article. James glanced at it and put it in his desk.

Some of the other boys at the seminary had begun giving him magazines and books that they said would help him understand the Church better. At first, James had been eager to read what they were giving him. But they didn't help him understand the Church any better; instead, those magazines and books confused him. They attacked the Church and James didn't know what to believe. Yet, he kept accepting the books and magazines. He hoped to read something that would clear up his confusion.

How can I know what's true? James wondered. *How can I know what's right?*

Among the books the other boys had given him were some novels. At first, James had left those aside. But as he grew more disturbed, he started to read the novels—

just to get his mind off his confusion. He began to enjoy the stories and to spend more time reading novels than studying. He realized that he didn't care much about school anymore.

He felt tired all the time. His grades began to sink. He even felt like he couldn't pray.

The priests on the staff saw that something was wrong. They tried to encourage James to study better, and he made some effort—but only a little.

"Your mother's here," a staff member told James one day. "She's waiting for you in the parlor."

Mamma Teresa was the last person James wanted to see right then. Dragging his feet, he walked to the parlor.

His mother lost no time in small talk. "What are you doing?" she asked, waving an envelope in the air. "We just received this letter about you. They say you're not studying. Your father isn't well and we have medical bills. Your brothers are working hard to pay Papa's expenses as well as yours, and you don't seem to care about anything. You don't seem to care about studying at all. What's the matter with you?"

All James could say was, "I don't know either, Mamma. I'll try to do better."

When Mamma Teresa left, James felt really discouraged. His mother had always understood him, but this time he knew she didn't. On the other hand, did he understand himself anymore?

On a Saturday morning in April, three days after James's sixteenth birthday, one of the priests called him into his office. "We're sorry, James," Father said. "You don't seem to want to be a priest anymore. You aren't giving a good example to the other boys, either. We've decided to send you home. Your father will come to pick you up this afternoon. Go pack your belongings."

James nodded and went to pack his things. He wasn't completely surprised. I've really lost interest in everything, he thought. I feel like I've been climbing an icy hill in the winter and sliding back. Now, I'm not even sure I want to climb that hill at all.

He was sure about one thing, though. Going home would not be pleasant.

How can I face Papa? he wondered. *Mamma? My brothers?*

Then he thought of Father John, who had helped him enter the seminary. *How can I face him*?

James suddenly wished that God would snatch him out of this confusing world and take him straight to heaven!

But he couldn't stand there thinking. His father was on the way. James packed up his belongings and brought them to the front door. Then he went back to his empty room and waited. He didn't go to lunch. He wasn't hungry at all.

Papa Michael greeted him with, "Well? Now you'll take up the hoe!" They loaded the ox cart, which the family always used to bring James to and from vacation. Then they rode home in silence.

At home, James kissed Mamma Teresa, who looked both hurt and angry. "Take your things up to your room," she said.

When his brothers came in for supper, they barely said hello, and during the meal everyone except Thomas ignored James.

After supper he went up to his lonely room on the second floor. *At least I still have a room of my own,* he thought. He had brought many books with him—mostly novels—and would be able to read until he fell asleep.

That night, though, James stayed awake for hours. Tomorrow was Sunday. He would have to see Father John. *Mary, my Mother,* he silently prayed, *help me get through that!*

Morning came much too soon for James. Much too soon also was the boys' departure for Mass with Papa Michael. As usual, Mamma Teresa had gone to an early Mass so she could prepare dinner.

During the two-mile walk, James lagged behind with Thomas. He watched his older brothers walking ahead with their father. Until now, he had hardly noticed that Juvenal, John, and even Francis were grown men.

They're strong, young farmers, James thought, *and what am I? I'm short and skinny, and I like to read. Where do I fit into this family? Where do I fit in anywhere?*

6

WHAT NEXT?

After Mass, James greeted Father John but didn't give him a chance to ask questions. Instead, he hurried home with his family.

The next day, the work week began. James went into the fields with his brothers but quickly grew tired and returned to the house. He went up to his room to read. Soon he was following this pattern every day.

A few Sundays later, Father John called James over to him as the Alberione family was leaving church. "Let's take a walk," he suggested kindly. As they walked, Father asked some questions, and James tried to explain what he had been going through. Little by little, the priest began to understand the situation. James had turned to a steady diet of novels in order to forget his confusion. But they had become part of his confusion! He seemed to have stopped looking for the truth.

"James," said Father quietly, "not everything is true or right just because you find it in a book or magazine. You have to judge what you read according to what can be trusted. To answer the questions you have in your mind right now, I have some books that can help you. Put the novels aside. Not all novels are good for you to read. Read the books I'll give you, and then we'll talk."

James went home with the books, but he didn't start to read them right away. He didn't seem to have energy for anything—either farm work or study.

A few days later, he was sitting lazily on the doorstep. The door was open, and Mamma Teresa came up behind him, clearly annoyed. "Either go to the fields or go to study!" she exclaimed. "If you stay here, I'll take my broom to you!"

James stood up. John, who was getting a drink of water from the well, said, "Come with me, James." After they had walked away from the house, twenty-one-year-old John spoke to his brother like a father to his son. "Listen, if you think you're good at studying, do it, and leave the farming to me. I can work hard enough for both of us."

Once again, realized James, *my family is trying to help me be the person God wants me to be.* As he watched his brother walk away,

James quietly prayed, "Thank you, Jesus, for giving me a family that supports me. Help me to study and learn what is true." For the next few weeks, he went to the fields in the morning, helped for a while, and then settled under a tree to study the books Father John had loaned him. His brother worked nearby, "hard enough for two."

When James returned the books to Father John, his confusion was gone.

"Now, tell me," Father asked, "what do you want to do with your life?"

James hesitated. Then he said, "I still think I'd like to be a priest. I mean, it's all I ever wanted to be. I can't picture myself as anything else."

Father John thought for a minute. Then he said, "That's good enough for now. I believe I can arrange a second chance for you."

A few days later, Mamma Teresa told James, "Father John was here yesterday and said that another seminary will accept you. It's the one he went to himself, in Alba. Your father and I talked it over last night, and Papa has agreed."

James felt quite overwhelmed—and very relieved.

That autumn Papa Michael and sixteen-year-old James climbed into the loaded ox cart. John came along to drive, because Michael Alberione wasn't feeling well.

When they reached the seminary in the city of Alba, some boys were outside playing a game. James heard one of them say, "Look at that! This boy's coming to study with a cow!"

James took the teasing remark calmly. *I'm going to make a fresh start,* he thought. *That's what matters.*

James soon discovered that life in the Alba seminary wasn't going to be easy.

He had trouble focusing. The priests at the seminary were watching his behavior, and James knew it. It was hard for him to sleep at night, so he was often sleepy during class and study time. He got upset easily. His classmates started to call him "Matchstick," because he would flare up quickly, like a lighted match.

All James's classmates except one received their cassocks that December.

Cassocks are long black garments with buttons down the front. At that time and place, priests and seminarians usually wore cassocks. A boy was not allowed to wear a cassock until he reached a certain point in his studies and the priests thought there was a good possibility that he could one day be ordained.

"You'll need to wait for *your* cassock, James," one of the priests said kindly.

"I understand," replied James. But it was hard to be different. James wanted to belong.

He couldn't have dreamed what would happen next.

7
A Mysterious Invitation

On the last night of 1900, the priests and seminarians of the Alba seminary went to the cathedral to pray for the needs of the Church and the world. There was Mass at midnight, followed by adoration of the Eucharist. Knowing that the Church was struggling with many problems, James prayed while kneeling before the Blessed Sacrament. He prayed for the people of the coming century.

Jesus, our world needs you so much. There are so many people who don't really know you. Lord, how can I help them? I want so much to lead people to you. Show me, Jesus, how you want me to do that.

James stayed on and on, losing all track of time. He felt in his heart that Jesus was asking him do something special to help the Church and the people of the new century that was beginning.

James left the cathedral around five o'clock in the morning. He was excited about what he felt Jesus was asking, and he

"It seemed that the Blessed Sacrament was surrounded by light and Jesus was speaking to me."

hurried back to the seminary. He ate a quick breakfast and went to his room, where he stayed most of the day—wondering and thinking about what had happened while he prayed at the cathedral.

Later, when he left his room for a minute, another seminarian asked, "Do you feel all right, James?"

"Sure—why?"

"You look excited, and you're very pale."

James tried to make a joke and hurried away.

A few days later, he told his friend Augustine (Uh-GUS-tin) about his experience. Augustine was the only other boy in James's class who wasn't wearing a cassock.

James tried to explain what that night had been like. "It seemed that the Blessed Sacrament was surrounded by light and Jesus was speaking to me. You know the words on the tabernacle in the cathedral? It seemed that Jesus was saying those words to me: 'Come to me, all of you.' I understood that he meant those words for everybody in the world."

Augustine listened quietly.

"But how can everybody come to Jesus?" James continued. "Many people have never heard of him. They have to be told. It would take a lot of people working together to bring the message of Jesus to the world."

"Missionaries do that," said Augustine.

"While I prayed the other night Jesus helped me understand that there's a new way to be a missionary," replied James. "There should be more books, magazines, and newspapers to spread the faith—many more. I think *that's* the kind of missionary work the world especially needs today. I think the Lord wants me to gather a group of people to print what the Church teaches and send or bring it everywhere."

"Wow," commented his friend. "Will you do that as a priest? Or will you leave the seminary?"

After thinking a minute, James said, "I'd still like to become a priest."

Soon after that, life became difficult for both boys. First, Augustine was called home because of family problems. Then, while Augustine was still away, Mamma Teresa wrote to ask James to help with the spring planting. He went home, wondering how long he would have to stay.

The next autumn, Augustine returned to the seminary and saw that James was missing. He wrote to his friend and was relieved to see him a few days later.

"I got your letter," James said. "I was already planning to come back."

"I'm going to receive my cassock this December!" Augustine exclaimed.

"I wonder if I will, too," James replied.

He soon found out that he *wasn't* going to receive a cassock.

Why are they making me wait? James wondered.

Augustine looked good in his cassock, and James was proud of his friend, who kept encouraging him not to give up. "I know it's hard not to wear a cassock when the rest of us have them," Augustine said, "but the cassock really isn't important."

"I guess you're right," James replied. "I can try to be a good seminarian whether I wear a cassock or not." James thought, *Augustine does everything well and says all the right things. I can learn so much from him.*

And then, Augustine got sick and had to leave the seminary.

Spring came, and again James's family called him home. *It seems that Papa and my brothers don't believe I really want to be a priest,* he thought. *Maybe they're worried I'll just end up coming home like before. But I don't want that to happen.*

While he worked in the fields with his brothers, he kept worrying about his future and about Augustine. Finally, he received a letter. Augustine had gotten worse and wanted to see him.

James went at once. He found Augustine lying in bed, very pale. His stepmother and his two sisters were sitting near him. It was painful to see the sick boy struggle to control the strong coughs that shook him from head to foot. Yet, when James said good-bye to his friend, he didn't realize he would never see him again.

James was still on the farm in early June, when he got word that Augustine had died. He couldn't believe it. The best friend he had ever had, with whom he had shared joys and sorrows, hopes and dreams!

James went to the funeral, where he saw all his seminary classmates with one of their professors, Father Francis Chiesa (Key-AY-suh). They were very kind to him, knowing what a shock this had been.

That June, James made a decision. *Augustine would never have turned back,* he thought. *I won't either. I'll do something special for God and the people of this new century. And I'll do it as a priest.*

8

The Hand at the Plow

"I'm so pleased," said Mamma Teresa. She was walking beside James as he carried his last bags to the waiting ox cart.

"Why, Mamma?"

"Because now you're sure what you want," his mother replied. "Your whole attitude is different. Everyone can see it."

By now, they had reached the cart where two of his brothers were waiting to drive him, so James merely smiled.

During the three-hour ride to Alba on that crisp autumn day, he kept thinking about what his mother had said. *It's true,* he thought. *A couple of years ago, I wished God would take me to heaven. Now I want to live, to become a priest, and to do something for the people of our time.*

A few days later, he spoke with Father Francis. "It was so strange," James said. "Each spring for the past two years, my family asked me to help on the farm. I wondered if it was a sign from God that I wasn't supposed to stay in the seminary.

Now I can't even understand why I thought that."

"It's good that you think differently now," replied Father. "Put it all behind you. But," he added with a twinkle in his eye, "you can't continue going home to help out each spring."

"Oh, no," laughed James. "That's over, and I've told them so. It's like what Jesus says in the Gospel. Someone who's plowing can't look back. For one thing, his furrow goes crooked. For another, he loses time. I want to go full speed ahead!"

Just as James's family had seen a difference in him that summer, so did the priests and seminarians. It was clear that James *did* want to go full speed ahead.

That December, he was permitted to receive the black cassock he had so wanted. Five more years of study remained before he could be ordained a priest.

Even though James had lost his best friend, those five years were happy ones. The seminary became the center of his life—his true home.

He had a new friend, too, in Father Francis. He had known the gentle priest for two years already and admired him very much. Now, Father Francis gradually became like a father to James, or even like an older brother. They were only ten years apart in age.

Father Francis was the seminary's spiritual director. It was his duty to help the seminarians understand how God was speaking to them through their personal experiences, through other people, and within their own hearts. A spiritual director is also called a spiritual father.

"I had a special experience, Father," James told him.

Father Francis listened carefully as James described that night in the cathedral. "I can see that God was speaking to you," the priest replied. "He has big plans for you. It's important to go ahead without letting anything tempt you to give up."

"I realize that now," James replied. "But it isn't clear to me what God is really asking me to do. So far, all I'm doing to get ready is studying history on my own. That helps me to understand the people of our time better. But I know how small I am in the face of a giant project like this. There must be many more things I should do to prepare myself."

"Keep on with the history for now," said Father Francis, "and, of course, be faithful to your seminary studies. God will help you understand his plan as time goes on."

Things were changing at the farm. John had left home to get married and start his own family. The year that James turned twenty, his father passed away. *Poor Papa,* James thought sadly. *He was a good man who had to live a hard life. I'm sorry that he and I didn't understand each other better.*

Juvenal, Francis, and Thomas continued to plant and harvest the crops. They no longer asked James to come home to help them in the fields. Instead, they welcomed him at vacation time and respected his need to spend much of his time praying and studying.

During the school year, James was very busy. He was taking classes on the Bible and theology. On Sundays he taught religion to children in two parishes. He tried to find ways to encourage families to have the Bible in their home and to read it. He even got some of his classmates to help keep the seminary clean!

James's professors asked him to organize a student discussion on an important subject, and he did. They asked him to substitute teach for several weeks when one of the professors became ill, and James did that, too. There was something about him that people were beginning to respect and admire. Although he was small and slim, when he taught or gave a talk he was full of energy and sure of what he was saying. His eyes shone with enthusiasm.

The bishop and the seminary staff didn't have any doubts about letting James become a priest.

He and ten of his classmates were ordained on June 29, 1907. James was twenty-three. The next day he celebrated his first Mass in his home parish of Saint Martin, where Father John was still pastor. How happy the older priest was!

Mamma Teresa and her other sons were present, as well as several other relatives. It was a day of great joy for all of them.

A whole new life was about to begin for Father James.

9

"This Must Be a Mistake!"

Father James Alberione rapped on the frame of the open door. "Good morning, Father Francis."

"Father James! Welcome back! How was your summer?"

Father James entered his friend's office and took the chair offered to him.

"It was great, Father. I stayed at Saint Martin's instead of at home and spent part of each day in parish work. I also studied for that college degree you feel I should get."

"Very good. I think that degree will be useful to you, since you want to run an organization that will publish books on our Catholic faith. True, you've studied theology for several years in the seminary, but a degree will make people pay more attention to you."

Father James frowned. "You know, it still isn't clear to me what the Lord wants me to do."

"Don't worry about it," said Father Francis. "God *does* want something, so he'll let you know more about it at the right time. Meanwhile, keep praying."

Father James settled down to the routine of the newly ordained priests of the Diocese of Alba. Besides celebrating Mass daily, the new priests devoted their weekdays to a final year of seminary studies. Every Saturday, each of them would walk to a country parish, usually several miles away, to stay overnight and help the pastor on Sunday.

That was the routine, but for Father James it didn't last long.

In March the bishop of Alba, Bishop Francis Re (RAY), sent for him.

"Father James, there's a parish that needs some help."

James waited, wondering what was coming next.

"The pastor in Narzole (Nar-ZOE-lay) is quite ill," the bishop continued, "and he has only one associate priest. I'd like you to go there and give a hand for a few months. Take your books along and continue your studies, too."

Pleased to help, Father James packed up his few belongings and went to Narzole.

Father Al, pastor of the church of Saint Bernard, was indeed very ill. From the associate pastor, Father Joe, Father James learned his duties and eagerly began to celebrate Mass and the sacraments. Right away, the people of the parish liked this small priest with the flashing eyes.

The days passed quickly, because there was so much to do. He even had to go to a university quite far away to take his special theology exam. When he passed, he received the title Doctor of Theology. Because of this, his friends would sometimes call him "The Theologian"—meaning a person who has studied much about God.

At the end of April, Father Joe told him, "You know, Father Al isn't the only person around here who's ill. I'm not well myself. I asked the bishop to let me retire. I told him you'll do fine without me. Today I received his reply. He's letting me leave the parish."

Father James swallowed hard. Now, with Father Al very ill, Father James would be the only priest serving all those families, and he hadn't even been ordained a year! Yet, it was an honor to be trusted so much. "Show me whatever else I need to know," he replied.

Father James carried on with all the responsibilities at the parish. One of the tasks that especially impressed him was hearing the confessions of dying people and giving them their last Communion.

So many deaths, Father James thought, *and yet so many births and Baptisms. The human race is like a great river. The river comes from little springs, which are the families, and flows along in a great flood until it empties into the sea of everlasting life with God. Will everyone reach that ocean?*

He thought of the mysterious invitation he had received eight years before. "Lord," he prayed, "I know it's important to give the sacraments to the living and the dying. But I think you want me to help the people of our time through books, magazines, and whatever else will be invented to spread information. How can I begin and when?"

One day, Father James had to go to Alba on parish business. He ran into John Gallo, one of the seminarians.

"How do you like it at Saint Bernard's?" John asked.

"I don't like being associate pastor," James replied frankly.

"So, you'd rather be pastor?"

"Much less."

John looked puzzled. "What would you like to do, then?"

Father James got a faraway look in his eyes. "I don't know yet. All I know is that I'd like to gather a lot of young people, sort of the way Don Bosco did, and teach them to write and print books and magazines about God."

In June, Father Al passed away, and a few weeks later a new pastor arrived. Father James was asked to stay on a little longer—to help and also to get some rest.

At the beginning of October, he received a letter from Bishop Re. When he opened it, he was shocked.

"No, it can't be!" he exclaimed. "This must be a mistake!"

"What's the matter?" asked the pastor.

"The bishop is asking me to become the spiritual director of the seminary! But I have no experience! I'm only twenty-four years old!"

10

God Is the Light

"I haven't made a mistake," Bishop Re told Father James. "You can do this. I have other duties for Father Francis and I need to replace him in this one. You had a hard time when you were a seminarian, so now you'll understand the problems of these young men and will be able to help them."

Father James didn't look convinced. Kindly, the bishop added, "Take a couple of days to pray over it."

"Thank you, Bishop," James replied. "I'll get back to you soon."

Father James prayed. He also went to Saint Martin's and talked with Father John. "The bishop has good judgment," said Father John. "He sees something in you that you don't see in yourself."

Back in Alba, Father James went to see Father Francis, who told him, "I was in my twenties myself when the bishop made *me* the spiritual director at the seminary."

"I don't want to give the wrong advice," James protested.

"Whenever you don't know what advice to give, tell the person you'll get back to him. Then pray for the right answer. If you're stuck, you can ask advice from one or more older priests without telling them why you are asking."

So Father James accepted the assignment and moved back into the seminary. Besides giving spiritual direction, he was asked to teach history, to oversee the seminary library, and to assist Bishop Re at his Sunday and feast day Masses. On weekends, as before, he helped out in the country parishes.

He also kept an eye on Joseph and Francis, two boys he had met at Narzole. Both wanted to be priests, but their families were poor. Because James spent little money on himself, he had enough to help pay both boys' seminary expenses.

"It's becoming clearer," Father James told Father Francis one day.

"You have a clearer idea about what the Lord wants you to do?"

"Yes! Instead of an organization of lay people, who could easily come and go—an organization that could even fall apart—I could start a congregation of religious priests and brothers. A religious congregation would hold together and be faithful to the teachings of the Church."

Father Francis nodded slowly and said, "I'm sure this idea came from the Lord, who does all things well."

Father James began learning about some of the religious orders and congregations in the Church. He wanted to know how the members of each of them lived and prayed.

He thought about the boys he had met in the parishes and invited to the seminary. By now, there were others besides Joseph and Francis. *Maybe some of these boys will join my congregation,* he thought.

Now that his idea was clearer, he talked about it with Bishop Re. "Bishop," Father James asked, "would it be unfair if I would eventually take a few seminarians away from the diocese and into the congregation I hope to start?"

"You're giving very much to the diocese every day," the bishop replied. "If a few young men want to join your congregation when the time comes, they may go with you."

Then Bishop Re paused. He knew that the young seminarians admired Father

James very much. A number of them might want to follow him. Half-joking, half-serious, the bishop added, "Just don't invite too many!"

Father James thought, planned, and waited. He couldn't start a congregation until he had work for the members.

Sometimes, he thought, *it's as if I'm half-blind, feeling my way along. But then light comes and I can see ahead a short distance. God is the Light. Right now, I'm back in the dark again, but the Lord will let me know when to begin my project. After all, it's really his project, not mine.*

On a September day in 1913, Father James gave a talk at one of the shrines in the city. The talk was about devotion to Mary. Bishop Re was present, and he came up to the young priest afterward.

"That was beautiful, Father James," said the bishop. "Your trust in Mary has helped me make a decision."

"Thank you, Bishop!" Father James replied. "May I ask what it was?"

"Yes. It involves you. I know that you belong to the Association of the Good Press."

Father James nodded. The Association of the Good Press was a group that wanted to make God better known by means of pamphlets, leaflets, and anything else that they could have printed.

The bishop continued, "Some of the other priests in the association would like you to direct the newspaper of the diocese."

"Really?" replied Father James, his heart beating faster and faster.

"I didn't like the idea," Bishop Re continued. "You already have more than enough work at the seminary and in the parishes. But now I realize that you rely very much on prayer to the Blessed Virgin. I think that somehow you'll manage to run the paper and still do your other work."

Father James felt like shouting, "Whoopee!" but instead he simply said, "Thank you, Bishop." His eyes were shining. It was time to start!

11

Beginning from Bethlehem

"You amaze me," a priest friend told Father James. "Even though you had to take some time off for your health, you've done wonders with the newspaper. I'm surprised, though, that you don't want that company to continue printing it. Why are you starting your own print shop?"

Father James smiled. "For some time I've wanted to open a little trade school, where boys can learn how to print good Catholic books."

He didn't mention that he hoped some of the boys in his school would become members of a religious congregation! Only Father Francis and Bishop Re knew about Father James's dream. It wasn't the right time to share it with anyone else yet.

On the evening of August 20, 1914, a teenage boy crossed a stone-paved city square in Alba, struggling with two bags of luggage. He approached the unmarked door of what looked like an ordinary business and knocked nervously. No answer. He knocked again, and the door opened suddenly.

"Oh!" the boy exclaimed. Stuttering, he said, "I-I-I'm looking for F-f-father James. I'm Des Costa."

"I know," smiled the old woman who had opened the door. "I was told you'd be coming. I'm the housekeeper. Father James is still out, but come in and I'll fix you some supper." She led Des inside and brought him into the kitchen.

While the elderly woman began to boil an egg and heat up some soup, Des sat down at the kitchen table and asked, "Is this really a s-s-school? Father J-J-James invited me t-t-to attend his school."

"It's going to be a trade school," replied the housekeeper. "Father says it will open very soon."

Just then, Father James came in. "Des, welcome! Come and see our print shop!" He led the boy into a big room to the left of the main door. There stood two printing presses and several smaller machines of different kinds. "My uncle, who has no family and manages a good business, helped buy this one," the young priest announced, patting a large secondhand press.

Des looked at the presses with interest. "Are these w-w-what the r-r-religious brothers will b-b-be running?" he asked.

"Someday," replied Father James. Then he added, "I once suggested that you become a brother, Des. But after praying more, I've begun to think that the Lord is calling you to be a priest. You can get rid of that stutter and preach sermons with the best of them. Ask the Blessed Mother to obtain this gift for you from her Son. Pray with faith."

"I *do* want to be a p-p-priest," Des replied. "I-I-I'll pray hard."

The next day Des walked to the seminary with Father James. The boy knew the place well. He had studied there for a year, until the staff had sent him home because of his stutter.

In the seminary parlor, Father James told him, "Wait here for Tor Armani (ahr-MAH-nee). He'll be coming soon. I don't think you've ever met him. He's been studying at another seminary."

A few minutes later, Des met Tor, who looked just a little older than himself.

"Are both of us going to stay with Father James this summer?" Tor asked.

"Well, yes, b-b-but I'm staying l-l-longer than that," Des replied. "You know about the t-t-trade school, don't you?"

"No, tell me," said Tor with interest.

Des told him the little he knew. Tor replied, "He asked me to spend the rest of the summer with him, but this isn't quite what I expected."

Father James came back and greeted Tor. He and Des helped Tor carry his bags to the print shop. Then Father James left, saying, "I have a lot to do at the seminary these days, but I'll be back every evening."

The two boys spent the next three days getting acquainted, helping the housekeeper in the garden next to their building, and simply wandering around the city.

On August 24, John Marocco (ma-ROH-coh) arrived. He was a young man a few years older than Tor and Des. "John will be your teacher," explained Father James. "Learn well, so you'll be able to teach the others. More boys will be coming."

Later that day, Father Francis and some of Father James's other friends arrived for the blessing of the presses and the building. First, Father James placed the shop under the protection of his favorite saint, the Apostle Saint Paul. Saint Paul was a person who did everything he could to tell people about Jesus and his love.

"Saint Paul went to many towns to preach about who Jesus is," Father James said. "He also wrote many letters that helped people understand the Church and how we are called to live what Jesus taught. Like Saint Paul we, too, will use what we print to teach people about Jesus."

Then Father James sprinkled holy water on the presses, the walls, and even the boys. After he blessed the school, they had a small celebration. The boys felt honored to be there among such serious adults. But they were still puzzled.

That night, Father James returned to his room at the seminary, leaving the boys with their new teacher. While John was unpacking, Tor and Des wandered into the print shop. "Are you g-g-going to be a p-p-priest?" asked Des.

"I hope so," the older boy answered. "Father James was paying my way at the seminary. But now I'm not sure what's going to happen."

In the following weeks, John began teaching Tor and Des about printing. Every afternoon Father James came to spend some time with them. Meanwhile, with the help of the boys and some hired workers, John was printing the newspaper for the diocese.

Soon a few other boys joined the little group. *Some of these boys will be our first members,* Father James thought. *Just as a stable was the birthplace of Jesus, so this print shop is the birthplace—the poor little Bethlehem—of our religious congregation. And because our work will be printing, our patron will be the Apostle Saint Paul.*

He told the boys they would continue their studies as soon as he could arrange it. They smiled, knowing that Father James would keep his promise.

12

THE SECOND STEP

"I want to start a second religious congregation," Father James announced. He was walking down a quiet street in Alba with Father Francis, who was now the pastor of Saint Damian's church. James looked sideways at the other priest to see his reaction.

Father James's spiritual director looked half-amazed, half-amused. "You haven't even started *one* yet," he reminded his younger friend. "You only have a group of boys whom John Marocco is teaching how to set type and print, while your friend Father Joseph Rosa teaches them how to live good Christian lives."

"No matter," Father James replied. His eyes sparkled like those of a mischievous child. "I want to start a congregation for *women*. Women can do much good in the Church. I've always felt that way, you know. I want a group of women to do the same work as our boys."

"And you think this idea to involve women in your project comes from God?"

Father James grew serious. "I really do."

"Well, let's both pray over it. We can talk about it again later."

Father Francis was always careful when Father James believed he had an inspiration from God. If it truly *was* an inspiration, nobody should interfere. It would be best to wait and pray.

As for Father James, he had been thinking of involving women in his project for several years, and now he was eager to start. But because of his friend's suggestion he continued to wait and pray.

When they discussed the matter again, Father Francis advised, "Go ahead."

Meanwhile, Father James realized that he needed a larger print shop, because more boys wanted to enroll in the school. He found a place and moved the shop, even though the boys still had to eat and sleep at their first location. After a while, with help from friends, James bought a large house on the outskirts of the city. As soon as it was ready, the boys moved in.

More and more pupils came, although some stayed only for a while. In those days, even city boys entered the working world very young. But they weren't ready for jobs that needed special training, such as printing. Many boys and their parents liked Father James's trade school, because the boys could be trained to hold a job that paid better than, for example, farming. Father James welcomed everyone, knowing that he was helping all of them to prepare for their future.

Often he told the boys how much good they were doing by printing for the Church. They were doing God's work with the "good press"—printing for a good purpose. He watched their reactions. Some boys smiled and nodded, their eyes glowing with happiness and excitement. *These are the ones who will stay,* thought Father James. *They'll be members of our congregation.*

But he was worried, too. He had asked his friend, Father Joseph Rosa, to teach the boys more about their faith and explain religious life to them. However, Father Joseph was not teaching them about religious life; he was teaching the boys how to live as faithful lay people.

Even though I have so much to do at the seminary, Father James thought, *I need to help prepare the boys who are interested in religious life. I'll begin as soon as possible.*

❖ ❖ ❖

One of the seminarians, Costanzo Merlo (Koh-STAHN-zoh MARE-loh), said, "I heard a rumor. If it's true, I think I should tell you about my sister, Teresa."

Father James gave the young man his full attention. He knew that Costanzo came from a good Catholic family. "Does Teresa want to be a sister?" he asked.

"Yes, she does, Father, but no convent will accept her—simply because she isn't strong. She's *never* been strong."

Father James knew how it felt to lack good health. "I'd like to meet her," he replied. "If she's interested, perhaps she could try spending a couple of weeks with the group we're forming."

On June 27, 1915, Teresa Merlo and her mother walked to Alba from the little hilltop village of Castagnito (Kah-stahn-YEE-toh) where they lived. They brought a couple of traveling bags in case Teresa decided to stay a few days.

At Saint Damian's church, Father Francis introduced them to Father James. First, Father James met with Mrs. Merlo in order to answer her questions about the congregation he was starting.

"I want to start a congregation of sisters who will write, print, and distribute books on our Catholic faith."

Then he spoke with Teresa.

"I've heard you're a good seamstress, Teresa," he began.

Teresa smiled. "My parents wanted me to be able to support myself, so they sent me to study sewing and embroidery."

"And you want to become a sister?" Father James asked.

"Yes, very much."

"Well, with us you could do both," replied Father James. "I want to start a congregation of sisters who will write, print, and distribute books about our Catholic faith. But right now, until we can begin, I've opened a sewing shop. There are three young women already working in it. Since Italy is now fighting in the Great War, we have a contract to make uniforms for soldiers. It's a temporary job, which will soon be replaced by the real work I have in mind."

Father James explained that he and Father Francis planned to give the young women instruction to prepare them to become religious sisters. Instead of running hospitals or schools or teaching in classrooms, this congregation of sisters would teach in a different way. They would write and print books and magazines about the Catholic faith. Father James hoped that in the future, they would also produce radio programs and films.

They would spread the good news that God loves the world so much that he sent his Son Jesus to die and rise to save us. "Saint Paul," he said, "had one love—Jesus Christ, and one burning desire—to bring him to everyone! You would be like him. The sisters will find ways to make Jesus known to everyone!" Father James's whole face lit up as he spoke. And he was pleased when Teresa's face lit up, too.

"All you have to do is obey," he said. "Would you like to try this out?"

"Yes, Father!" Teresa said joyfully.

13

SLOWLY BUT STEADILY

"Sometimes I worry about you," Father Francis remarked to Father James. "You celebrate Mass at the seminary, preach the morning meditation to the seminarians, teach there for several hours, and give spiritual direction. Then, in the afternoon, you drop in at the young women's sewing shop, direct the newspaper, and teach the boys. I won't mention the other kinds of things you're always getting involved in."

"You're quite involved yourself," replied Father James with a smile. "You're still teaching at the seminary, and now you're also giving Bible reflections, classes, and advice to our growing group of young women. Thanks to you, they know the Catholic faith really well. I'm very grateful for that. I couldn't have looked after both groups by myself."

"Well," Father Francis explained, "like you, I've prayed a lot to know what God is asking. I believe the Lord wants this. Since I was already training religion teachers for my parish, it wasn't hard to instruct these young women, too."

Three of the young women were adults—Teresa, Angela, and Clelia (CLAY-lee-uh). They had already told Father James and Father Francis that they hoped to become religious sisters. The rest were teenagers, who came to learn sewing. Most of them moved on after a few weeks or months and were replaced by others.

By now, the sewing shop had a second purpose. It was helping the trade school produce religious books. The boys would bring over stacks of folded sheets of paper that had already been printed and needed to be sewn together in sets as the next step in bookbinding.

"It's not easy to sew this stiff paper," said one of the teenage girls.

"That's true," Teresa agreed. Then she reminded the little sewing group, "But we're doing the Lord's work. We're helping to make books that will teach many people about God,"

"I'm glad we have this new place to work in," said Angela. "That first print shop where the boys had worked was pretty greasy for a sewing shop."

Clelia added, "It's good, too, that now we're living together as a community, instead of with separate families. We'll begin now to know what our life will be like as religious sisters."

At that point, everything was going quite well for both little communities. But Father Francis was right about Father James's schedule. It was heavy for the young priest, and often he had to take a day to rest, just so he could keep going. Father James's health had never been good, and it got no better as he tried to keep up with all his duties.

One of Father James's hidden tasks was cooking. He wasn't much of a cook, but many times he and the "boys of Saint Paul," as people called them, prepared their own supper. Father James would make a soup of whatever was available and stir it as he taught the boys some basic seminary subject. After he had found a still larger house for the boys and moved in with them, he also prepared their breakfast while they were out at Mass. Meanwhile, he continued all his regular duties at the seminary.

Another extra task Father James had taken on was writing to the seminarians who had been drafted to serve in the army. War had been raging since 1914. Many young men, including seminarians, had been drafted. The seminarians were far from home and lonely. Father James sent them letters of advice and encouragement very often, sometimes weekly.

Meanwhile, he worried that the boys in his own little community needed to study more of the basic seminary subjects than he himself had time to teach them. One day he realized, *I don't have to do all of this myself. Joseph is the answer!*

During Father James's first year as a priest, he had met Joseph Giaccardo (JEE-uh-CAR-doh) in Narzole and had helped him enter the seminary. Now, Joseph was a twenty-one-year-old seminarian. Father James had always hoped that this young man would become one of his helpers. *It has to be his choice, though,* Father James thought. *He has to freely choose to join us.*

Father James began dropping hints. Joseph hesitated. The young man admitted that he was worried. If he went to live with Father James's little community, would he be able to finish his studies at the seminary?

Joseph had wanted to be a priest for a long time. He didn't want to lose his chance.

The seminarian went to talk with Bishop Re, but the bishop wouldn't give him any advice. "This has to be your decision," Bishop Re told him.

Joseph took all his concerns to Jesus in prayer. *Jesus, I am torn,* he prayed. *I want so much to be a priest. I also feel like you are calling me to Father James's new community to serve you through the work of printing books and newspapers. Help me to know what you want me to do. Shall I stay here at the seminary or shall I ask to join the new community?*

After several anxious weeks and lots of prayer, Joseph knew what to do. He declared that he wanted to join Father James's community no matter what. Soon after that, he felt a great peace.

"This will work out fine," Father James told his young friend. "It's all settled. Starting this summer, you'll live with the boys of our community, but during the school year you'll help at the seminary as my teaching assistant. You'll fit in your other classes as well. In the evenings, you can teach our boys."

Joseph was overjoyed. That summer, he went to live with the growing community.

He started right away to proofread. It was an important job, because there could be serious mistakes in the printed sheets called proofs.

In those days, printing was done by means of raised metal letters—letters that were backwards so that paper pressed against them would show the letters printed in the correct position. (Think of a rubber stamp.) People who set type for printing could make mistakes easily, since they always had to read backwards. It was easy to confuse "d" and "b," for example. Before a press began to print hundreds of copies, a proof was made. This was a sample printed sheet, which had to be read carefully, to "prove" that everything was in the right place.

Father James had been spending many hours reading proofs. Now Joseph would help him with this, and with much else.

"This is where I belong," sighed Joseph. He had found his place in life.

14

A Grain of Wheat

"I feel so bad about this," said one of the boys to Father James. The boy's name was Bart, and Father James looked forward to the day when Bart would be ordained a priest. Bart continued, "Here I am, about to pronounce my religious vows with the others, while Maggiorino (MAH-jor-EE-noh), who entered the day before I did, can't because he is so sick."

"Maggiorino is too young to make his vows anyway," said Father James. "But I agree that it's a sad situation. Maggiorino has his heart set on becoming a full member of our congregation, but it may not happen. Let's keep him in our prayers."

Bart was preparing to make his religious vows in the ceremony of religious profession. All the boys were eager to attend this ceremony, which would be the first ever to take place in their community. After the ceremony Bart would be a religious brother.

Father James was happy, too. He thought, *God has sent us boys and young men who want to make religious vows. The fact that the Lord has sent them here is a sign that he himself is pleased with us, even though some people are not.*

Some lay people and priests had begun to criticize Father James for gathering teen-age boys to print books and young women to help bind them. "What are those young people doing?" they asked. "Printing is no job for teenage boys or young ladies. Father James should know better." They complained to Bishop Re. Some even wrote to the Pope in Rome.

But the bishop knew Father James well and trusted him. So did Father Francis. Both of them stood by James and refused to believe the unkind gossip. They had both seen first-hand the way the whole community worked together and how much good Father James was teaching them to do through the printed word. The bishop wrote to the Vatican to tell Church officials that Father James was a good and wise priest.

The day for the profession ceremony was December 8, 1917. It was the feast of the Immaculate Conception of Mary. Because the community didn't have a chapel yet, a statue of Mary Immaculate was placed in the best room of the house. That evening, standing beside the statue, Father James spoke to all the boys.

"From the very first day," he said, "our community has had to go through many difficulties. The fact that we've come through all these is a sure sign that God has desired this community and our work from the beginning." He encouraged the boys never to give up their vocation.

Then, one by one, four young men made their religious vows. The four were Joseph, Des, Bart, and Michael. Far away in the army, on the same day and about the same time, Tor was also making his religious profession.

At that time many religious priests, brothers, and sisters changed their names when they made their vows to show that they had begun a new life. Joseph and Tor took the names Timothy and Titus, after two of Saint Paul's helpers. Bart took Paul, and Michael took Dominic. Des—who had overcome his stuttering—took the name of a great preacher-saint, Chrysostom (KRIS-uh-stuhm). From this day forward these young men would be called by their new names.

"I'm worried," Father James told Father Francis a few weeks later. "Even though the war is almost over, the draft board wants me to report. They need more soldiers to replace those who have been wounded."

"If the government calls you into the army," his friend replied, "Bishop Re will be sure your two groups are taken care of."

"I know," said James. "The bishop told me that. But there are so many little things to look after! I've asked everybody to pray. Oh, by the way—the young women have even promised the Lord that if I'm not drafted they'll make a large rug for the sanctuary of your church."

"I'll look forward to receiving the rug. Go with faith."

Men had to report to the draft board in regular clothes. Father James no longer had any, so he borrowed a shirt, pants, a jacket, and a cap from various boys his size.

Without his cassock, Father James looked very small and terribly thin. The people at the draft board took one look at him, shook their heads in amazement, and sent him home. As he walked away, James could hear one of them commenting, "Did you see *that* one? It's a wonder he has enough strength to walk. He's nothing but skin and bones!"

On his way back, still wearing the borrowed clothes, Father James opened the door of the women's sewing shop and poked his head inside. "Tell Teresa they didn't take me," he said.

"Who was *that*?" asked a girl who was helping in the shop.

"That was Father James!" Teresa exclaimed, coming from the back room. "Let's get to work! We promised the Lord we'd make a rug for Saint Damian's!"

In June of that year—1918—more happy events took place, and in July a sad one.

In a private ceremony on June 29, the Feast of Saints Peter and Paul, Teresa, Angela, and Clelia made their first vows. Now they were religious sisters! They looked forward to the day when they could make perpetual vows, which meant that they would be religious sisters for the rest of their lives. That same day, Father James celebrated Mass in the boys' own house, in a room they had turned into a chapel. James had hired craftsmen to build a wooden altar. From then on, the boys wouldn't need to go out for Mass.

That same month, Maggiorino, who had been home recovering from a serious sickness, came back to spend a few hours with Father James and all his old friends. Everyone was happy to see him. He didn't look well, however, and couldn't stay long. About three weeks later, in mid-July, the community was saddened to hear that Maggiorino had gotten sick again, and that this new illness had taken his life.

All of them went to their friend's funeral in the little hill town of Benevello (BEN-i-VEL-oh). On their way, Brother Timothy remarked to Brother Paul, "When he knew he was going to die, Maggiorino said he would offer his life for all of us who are spreading the message of Jesus through the printed word, I believe it's like what Jesus said in the Gospel. The seed falling to the ground and dying will give a rich harvest."

Quietly Brother Paul replied, "I wonder if someday the Church will call Maggiorino a saint—a patron saint for young people."

15

Challenges

On an October afternoon of that year, Father James dropped in on the three religious sisters at the bookshop they had recently opened.

"We need to talk about something," he said. Leaving a young helper out front to look after the shop, all four gathered in the back room.

"Our Lord is offering you a beautiful opportunity to do good," Father James began. "The bishop of Susa has heard about you and is asking for your help. He wants you to take over the diocesan newspaper there—setting type, printing, and mailing. Do you think you can do it for a few years?"

The three were startled. Susa was at the foot of the Alps, mountains barely visible on the horizon. The city was more than 140 kilometers (eighty-eight miles) away—a long distance by train. But what really worried the young sisters was their lack of training.

Father James broke the silence. "What answer can I give to Bishop Castelli (Cah-STELL-ee)? He asked for you. Will you go?"

Angela spoke for all three. "Father, you know how few we are and what we're able to do. Only Emilia knows how to set type, and even she knows very little. How will we be able to do this?"

"You can come to the boys' print shop and learn," replied Father James. When the sisters remained silent, he added, "Jesus, Mary, and Saint Paul will help you."

The three looked at each other. Suddenly they all began talking at once.

"Yes, Father!"

"Yes!"

"We'll go!"

The sisters wanted to begin preparing right away, but the strongest of them, Clelia, suddenly fell sick. As they waited for her to recover, Angela began to learn how to set type. Teresa started printing. "Clelia will probably do most of the printing," Teresa said to Angela. "She's much stronger than I am. I can simply replace her when there's a need."

But Clelia's sickness got worse. It was the Spanish flu, which swept through Europe at the end of World War I. More people died of the Spanish flu in one year than during all four years of the war. On October 22, Clelia told Father James, "If the Lord spares me, I want to give all my energy to spreading Jesus's message through the printed word. And if I have to die, I offer my life for the same purpose."

Clelia *did* die. She passed away that same evening, while the sisters and the teenage girls were praying the Rosary around her bed.

Now there were only three who would go to Susa: two sisters—Sister Teresa and Sister Angela—and Emilia, who was still a teenager. They had lost the strongest member of their group. Still, they trusted in God and were determined to go to Susa.

They left in December by train. Sister Angela went a few days before the others, together with Brother Paul, who was going to help prepare the print shop and then return to Alba. Sister Teresa and Emilia followed, with two more girls who had recently joined them.

"Only five," said Brother Timothy, as Sister Teresa's train pulled out of the station.

"They'll do all right," replied Father James. "They can't trust in themselves, so they'll trust in God."

That Christmas, the little community in Alba had a scare.

According to the custom of the times, Father James celebrated midnight Mass in the chapel, followed by two other Masses. Then, after a simple meal, everyone went to bed.

Suddenly Father James heard a cry from the street below: "Fire! Fire!" He jumped out of bed, looked out the window, and saw the daughter of the print shop's janitor. She was shouting and pointing down the street. James dressed quickly and told the first boy he found, "It's the print shop! Wake everybody up! Tell the older ones to come with me and the younger ones to go to the chapel and pray!"

They ran down the street to the print shop, which was filled with smoke. Father James led the way in, searching for the fire to put it out. He stumbled in the dark, fainted from the smoke, and was carried to safety by the janitor's son. Meanwhile, the

"Fire! Fire!"

firemen arrived and discovered that the fire had already burned out. Only smoke and soot remained.

Sparks had escaped from the wood stove and landed on a pile of paper, which had gone up in flames. The fire had also damaged the nearby machines.

Father James and the boys spent the rest of the night airing out the shop and trying to clean up.

The next day, a friend of Father James stopped by to speak with him.

"I was so sorry to hear about the fire," he said. He glanced around. "So much soot! You must be sad to see all this damage. Even your windows are broken from the heat."

Standing in the midst of the mess, Father James declared, "It's all right. Any sin is more serious than this."

"How are they doing in Susa?" Father Francis asked in the spring of 1920.

"The newspaper's coming out fine," Father James replied. "Of course, the sisters' living quarters are poor. Yet, people *did* help them, when they had a fire there soon after our own here. They're managing, and everyone is happy—that's what counts. Girls are asking to enter the community and they have a bookshop."

"They must be praying well."

"I think so. We sent them copies of our new prayer, the one we call the Pact. It helps all of us remember how much we need God's help." He smiled. "By the way, the Susa sisters have a nickname. Because of the big picture of Saint Paul in their bookshop, some people have started to call them the 'Daughters of Saint Paul.' I rather like it, don't you? Maybe that should be their official name."

"It sounds good. How's everything going here?"

"Better. Now that Father Timothy has been ordained, he has more time for teaching the boys. But our newest living quarters still aren't large enough. So many young men want to enroll in the trade school that I'm buying a large piece of land to build on. I only wish the bishop would free me from my seminary duties. We're really growing."

"Well," his friend replied, "you *did* ask the bishop, so he may free you one of these days."

Yes, that would happen soon—but not in the way Father James expected.

16

RIDING OUT THE STORM

On a warm July morning in 1920, Father Francis looked up from his desk in Saint Damian's rectory. He heard the housekeeper answer the front door and recognized Father James's voice. "Come in, Father James," he called.

The younger priest entered. He looked more upset than he had in years.

"Easy, easy, James," said Father Francis. "Sit down and take a deep breath."

Father James sank into a chair. His eyes, which usually shone or flashed, were brimming with tears.

"Calm down," urged the older priest. "Take your time." To make it easier, he asked, "Is this about the seminarians who've asked to join your boys?"

Father James nodded. "I've just come from the bishop. He thinks I've been using my role at the seminary to lead those eight older seminarians into my community. But I haven't! All these years I've invited only a few, as the bishop and I had agreed. Except for Timothy, they were always younger boys, like Paul when he came. I've actually discouraged many others. I asked the older seminarians only to pray for our work."

"So you told that to the bishop," Father Francis replied.

Father James nodded again. "But I'm not sure he believed me. He said he's setting me free from my duties in the diocese so I can be with my community full time. Of course, I had asked for exactly that, but the way this has happened is hard to take. I love the diocese."

"Of course. This is hard for you but also hard for the bishop. He's losing eight promising young men, who soon would have been priests in parishes. As for you, you're afraid you've lost the friendship of the bishop and perhaps some of the priests. Father James, both you and the bishop need to ride out this storm. Time can calm everything—and everyone."

After talking with his friend a little longer, Father James left the rectory and began to walk home. *Father Francis is right,* he reflected. *This problem came up like a sudden storm, and took all of us by surprise.*

As he walked, Father James decided that when the eight young men—now on summer vacation—would come to join his boys, each must be welcomed warmly. He didn't want them to feel bad about what had happened. After all, none of them had done anything wrong. They hadn't even known about one another's decisions.

As for what to do next—as usual, Father James headed for the chapel to talk to the Lord. *Jesus,* he prayed, *I've always come to you to ask what to do. Help me to do what you want. Please help the bishop understand that I love the diocese and am only trying to make you better known in the Church and the world. Please bless the young men who want to join us.*

One by one, the eight young men entered Father James's growing community. They settled in and began to learn typesetting, proofreading, and printing. When the school year began in the fall, they continued with the classes they would have taken in the seminary. Their main teacher was Father Timothy, who was now working toward a theology degree, as Father James had before him.

"I'm worried," one of new members told Father Timothy one day. "Do you think the bishop might not ordain us when we're ready? Will we have to move to Pisa (PEE-suh)? I heard that the cardinal of Pisa wants us there very much."

"It's true that we've been invited to Pisa," replied Father Timothy. "But we might not go. Father James has been writing to some of Bishop Re's advisors, explaining the situation. And, of course, Father Francis will also speak for us to the bishop."

As the months passed, everything did calm down, just as Father Francis had said it would. A large building began to go up on Father James's new property at the edge of the city. It was a sign that Father James hoped to stay in Alba.

When the building was finished, machines were brought in to fill the first floor. Father James, Father Timothy, and all the young men and boys moved into the upper floors.

On October 5, 1921, excitement filled the air at the community's new home. The bishop had come to see the building and bless it. He had also been invited to a special ceremony. That day Father James, Father

Timothy, and several others made their perpetual profession of vows, while still more young men made their first vows. They began to call their community the Society of Saint Paul.

The Society of Saint Paul still needed official Church approval, but they had taken another step on the way. Father James was truly in the process of founding a religious congregation. His followers had already begun to think of him as "the Founder."

17

"WHERE AM I LEADING THEM?"

Almost as soon as the new building was finished, Father James realized that it was again too small. So many boys were coming! He decided to add a second building to the first—one just like it. However, the contractor needed a down payment for materials.

Father Timothy was in charge of the community's money. "We can't afford the down payment," Father Timothy told Father James. So the Founder, who had been gathering more sisters, asked the sisters to pray for the exact amount needed.

A day or so later, a poorly dressed woman walked into the large building of the Society of Saint Paul and began climbing the stairs. Meanwhile, Father James was coming down. When they met, the unknown woman handed the priest an envelope, turned around, and left without saying a word. The envelope contained the exact amount of money the contractor needed! Father James went to the chapel and asked the Lord to bless the generous woman who had helped them. Soon they began to build.

In the summer of 1922, Father James invited the sisters from Susa to come back to Alba for a few weeks and meet the new group of young women he had been gathering. They were going to become one congregation. The nickname from Susa would become their official name: Daughters of Saint Paul.

There were nine sisters in all. They made a week-long spiritual retreat, renewed their religious vows, and took new names. Teresa Merlo was now called Sister Tecla (TEK-luh), after a disciple of Saint Paul.

"From now on," said Father James, "Sister Tecla will be your superior, the sister in charge of your community."

He asked the sisters from Susa to return there and spend the following year training other people to run the newspaper. Afterward, they would close the house in Susa and return to Alba.

The Society of Saint Paul and the Daughters of Saint Paul were full of life and energy—except for Father James. Although he was only in his late thirties, Father James was becoming weak and had to rest often. Most food didn't agree with him, and his throat was often sore.

In June of 1923, several months into his illness, he received sad news from his brothers Juvenal and Thomas. Their mother was dying. James went to say good-bye to Mamma Teresa, the family member who had understood him best. He arrived just in time.

The night following Mamma Teresa's burial, Father James was back in Alba with the community. He took a long walk alone on a ridge outside the city. The boys, young men, and sisters watched him from a distance, wishing they could take away some of his pain.

A few days later, on a hot Sunday afternoon, the Founder walked to a town some distance from the city. Following the custom of the times, he preached in the parish church that evening. In the twilight chill, he walked back to Alba and immediately went to bed with a terrible cough. Father James was seriously ill, and a doctor was called. That doctor soon sent for two others.

"It's what we've warned him about for years," one of the doctors explained to

Father Timothy. "He's been working so hard and not taking care of himself, and now he has a very serious illness. Father James has tuberculosis (too-BUHRK-yoo-LOH-sis)."

In those days, people often *died* of tuberculosis. Even if they lived, they usually had to spend the rest of their lives in a rest home with a great deal of help and care.

Word spread swiftly through the Society of Saint Paul, the boys of the trade school, and the Daughters of Saint Paul. What would they do if they lost their Father and Founder? All began to pray hard for his recovery.

Father James himself was stunned. "What can I do?" he asked Father Francis, who had hurried to be with him. "I can't leave all this in Father Timothy's hands. It's too much." He looked at his friend. "Could *you* . . . ?"

Alarm flickered in Father Francis's usually calm eyes. He swallowed hard but answered quietly, "I'm willing."

A few days later, Father James told him, "I've talked to Father Timothy and we're making plans for you to take over, with his help. But it doesn't have to happen immediately. Father Al in Benevello has invited me to stay with him in the hope that I can last a little longer. The air there is very good. It's summer, and Father Timothy may be able to handle everything by himself for a few months. After that. . . ."

Slowly, the horse and cart made their way up into the hill country. Sister Teresa Raballo (Rah-BAH-loh), seated beside the Founder, glanced back to see the buildings of Alba growing smaller beyond the patchwork of green, brown, and golden fields.

"Are we almost there?" she asked.

"It's quite a distance yet," replied Father James weakly.

"Yes, it's much farther still," agreed the driver.

The Founder had gone to Benevello to rest before, but always alone. Now, because Father Al's housekeeper was elderly, Father James was bringing Sister Teresa to look after him. She was good at both housework and cooking.

As they continued their slow journey, Father James wondered what would happen to his community if he died or had to retire to a rest home.

Father Francis and Father Timothy are both very good priests, he thought. *Yet, I don't think the two of them will be able to take care of everything. Father Francis is more of a thinker than a man of action. Father Timothy is better as a right-hand man than as a leader.*

Lord, he asked silently, *where am I leading all those young people? Do I have to abandon them partway down the road? Will this be a dead end for all of us?*

18

A Dream

For the first two weeks that Father James stayed at Benevello, he was too sick to do anything. "His fever is very high," Sister Teresa told Father Al one day. "I bring him only the little bit of food that he can keep down. Then I leave him to rest and pray."

"And you spend your time helping my housekeeper, who's so far up in years," said Father Al. "She's grateful for that and so am I."

"Well, I'm young and strong, after all," replied Sister Teresa.

After those first gloomy weeks, on some days the Founder's fever went down a little; on other days it was back up. On the days that his temperature was almost normal, he would go to the church and spend a few hours of the afternoon in prayer. He also began to eat more. Father James started to write a set of rules for the Society of Saint Paul. He wanted to obtain the Church's official approval for the congregation, and a rule of life would be needed for that.

Soon Father James was celebrating Mass daily again. "Since I haven't had a fever for a few days, may I go to Alba?" he asked.

Travel arrangements were made, and to the joy of his two communities, he met them in the chapel to greet them and give them encouragement. "I had a dream," he said. "In that dream Jesus told me something that's good for all of us."

Everyone listened eagerly.

"He said, 'Do not be afraid. I am with you.'"

His listeners recognized the two sentences. They can be found at various places in the Bible, but usually not together. The young people realized that, placed together, those two sentences were very encouraging. God was telling them he would be with them no matter what happened. Even if something happened to Father James, God was with them!

Father James continued, "And then Jesus said, 'From here I want to give light.' I believe that Jesus means these words for all of us. He wants to give light to us and to all people." By "light" the Founder meant truth and understanding. As he said this, he gestured toward the tabernacle, where Jesus was present in the Blessed Sacrament. From the tabernacle, Jesus would inspire the Society of Saint Paul and the Daughters of Saint Paul, who would bring his message to the world.

"But also," the Founder continued, "Jesus said that we must be sorry for our sins."

Father Timothy always took notes when Father James gave a talk, so he was writing now. "We should post these words in our chapel," he whispered to himself. "These are God's special words to our communities. We must never forget them."

The Founder said good-bye and returned to Benevello. A few weeks later, he was back in Alba again—but this time to stay!

The doctors were puzzled and amazed. They examined Father James, but couldn't find any trace of tuberculosis. Soon all the members of the Society of Saint Paul and the Daughters of Saint Paul were saying there had been a miracle.

Father James didn't deny that he had been cured in a wonderful way. "I was cured through the help of Saint Paul," he explained. "Saint Paul is the real father and founder of our congregations. Saint Paul will always pray for us!"

"Am I relieved!" exclaimed Father Francis. "You've always talked about teaching the Catholic faith by using radio and movies and all sorts of things besides the printed word. I have no idea how to do any of that. I'm glad I don't have to worry about it any longer!"

Father James's eyes twinkled. "I was wondering how I could ever explain to you and Father Timothy all the ideas that Jesus keeps giving me! I have so many projects swarming around in my head."

He stopped, then added, "By the way, do you remember the dream I told you about last month?"

Father Francis nodded.

"Father Timothy has already posted the words in our chapel."

By the end of that year, 1923, there were ten priests in the Society of Saint Paul. The seminarians who had entered in 1920 had been ordained! These younger priests were helping Father James and Father Timothy teach the boys. Meanwhile, the Founder was also working to get official Church approval for the Society. By now, the congregation was made up of priests, religious brothers who did not intend to become priests, and boys who wanted to become one or the other.

Father James continued to write the rule of life for the members of the Society of Saint Paul. He told them that they would honor Jesus as the Divine Master and Teacher and Mary as the Queen of Apostles. Saint Paul would continue to be their patron saint.

One day Father James told Sister Tecla, "I've prayed about this and I believe that God is asking us to start a group of sisters with a special vocation to prayer." He had been thinking about this for years, and now the time had come. On February 10, 1924, eight Daughters of Saint Paul became the first members of the new group. They were called the Disciples of the Divine Master. The Founder chose a young sister named Ursula Rivata (Ree-VAH-tah) to be their first superior. He gave her the name Sister Scholastica (Skoh-LAS-ti-kuh), after a great saint known for her deep prayer life.

Father James's new buildings were located on several acres of land. To save on expenses, the members had begun to grow crops—especially potatoes and cabbages—and to pasture cows, which provided them with milk. They also cut expenses by starting their own oven for making bricks, so more buildings could be erected. They even started a paper mill to make paper for printing and encouraged friends to plant fast-growing trees, so there would be a supply of wood for paper-making.

From all over Italy, teenage boys and girls were coming to Alba to enter the Society, the Daughters of Saint Paul, and the Disciples of the Divine Master, They needed a much larger chapel. In fact, they needed a *church*.

To raise funds for the church, Father James turned to lay people who helped the Society of Saint Paul by working with them or giving money. These were the Pauline Cooperators. "Most religious congregations have a group of lay people who work with them," Father James had explained. "The Cooperators can help us do much more good." The building of the church of Saint Paul would be an important project for the Pauline (PAUL-lyne) Cooperators. It would take three years to build and even longer to finish inside.

While construction of the church began, other things were also happening.

19

Branching Out

On a cold January evening in 1926, Father James and Father Timothy came from the chapel and walked toward the street, followed by an excited crowd of younger members. Father Timothy and fourteen of the boys wore jackets and were carrying luggage. They were going to take the train to Rome to open a new house! Shivering, the others walked a short distance with them, saying good-bye to their friends. Suddenly the Founder stopped and asked Father Timothy to bless all of them. Father James knelt down in the snow, and everyone else did the same.

"*You* should bless *us*!" exclaimed Father Timothy, but he didn't have a choice. The Founder remained kneeling, so the younger priest blessed the group.

Father James rose and gave Father Timothy a quick good-bye hug. The young people parted from their friends. While the travelers headed for the station, the others hurried inside to get out of the cold.

A few days later, a Daughter of Saint Paul named Sister Amalia (Uh-MAHL-yuh), and fourteen teenage girls also took the train for Rome.

For several years, the Society and the Daughters of Saint Paul lived in very poor rented apartments, until they could afford to buy property.

Meanwhile, the communities in Alba continued to grow.

One day, two girls who hoped to become Daughters of Saint Paul were talking in the shipping room as they wrapped bundles of Mass pamphlets for mailing.

"I don't understand," said the newer girl. "If the Society had to be approved by the bishop before it could be approved by the Pope, why couldn't Bishop Re have done it right away? He likes us, right?"

"It doesn't work like that," explained the older girl. "If a bishop wants a congregation in his diocese, he has to ask permission from the Vatican before he can approve it himself. That's the way things are."

"Well," replied the first girl, "I'm glad the waiting is over, anyway. Now that the

Society has been approved by the bishop, we Daughters of Saint Paul and the Disciples of the Divine Master should be next."

"Hopefully one day soon we'll all also have the approval of the pope, so we can go to the whole world, just as the Founder says," added the older girl.

Just then the Founder came by.

"What are you doing?" Father James asked them.

"Making packages of Mass pamphlets," replied the younger girl.

The Founder stopped. "No," he said. "You're doing much more than that. You're teaching people what the Mass is all about! *You're a teacher with many pupils.*"

He moved on, and the girls looked at each other. The older one turned red. "Sometimes I forget the real meaning of what we're doing," she said. "And I also forget that if we pray together or silently while we're working, God will use our prayers to help the pamphlets do more good."

Several more months passed before the Daughters of Saint Paul received their own approval from the diocese. Even though they rejoiced when approval did come, Father James and Sister Tecla were sad, because the Disciples of the Divine Master hadn't been approved as well. "We'll try again later," the Founder said.

That spring, the Daughters of Saint Paul began something new. Carrying packages of books, they went out two by two to visit families in their homes. By doing this, they reached people who had never come to the bookshop. Father James was pleased with this new way of helping God's word reach those who needed it. He began to send Daughters of Saint Paul to open bookshops in other cities in Italy. They went with a supply of books but very little money. "This is the way to start out," Father James explained. "Always begin from Bethlehem—poor, as Jesus was." Each time, the sisters had to find living quarters and locate a place for a book center (another name for a bookshop). Meanwhile they supported themselves by going door to door, offering people the books they had brought from Alba. The books were not too expensive and the families were eager to have good books to read.

In 1931, the Founder took another step. He began to send Society of Saint Paul priests across the Atlantic by steamship. They went to Brazil, Argentina, and the United States without knowing Portuguese, Spanish, or English. "You'll learn the language there," Father James told them. The Pauline priests went with almost no money. They trusted that God who was calling them to these new lands would provide for them. The Founder hoped that within a few months he could send the Daughters of Saint Paul and the Disciples of the Divine Master to the same countries.

20

More Steps

In 1933, Bishop Re retired. The following year he passed away.

"Bishop Re did so much for me," Father James remarked to Father Francis. "When I was a seminarian and young priest, he gave me difficult assignments. But those assignments—especially as spiritual director—made me better prepared to found our congregations. And later, he helped us get official approval."

"It's true," replied Father Francis. Then he added, "When we look back, we can see the hand of God. You wouldn't have been ordained in Bishop Re's diocese if you hadn't been expelled from that first seminary in another diocese."

"I know," agreed James. "Being sent home seemed like such a tragedy then, but Alba was the best place for us to begin. Yes, God's ways are amazing."

The Founder continued to send out priests, brothers, and sisters to cities in Italy and beyond—as close as France and as far away as China. Meanwhile, he himself was writing books. The priests and brothers in Alba were busily printing magazines for children, families, and parishes. Father Chrysostom traveled up and down Italy by motorcycle, telling bishops and priests about the work of the Society of Saint Paul. In Rome, the Society was printing Bibles in different languages.

The Daughters of Saint Paul were very active as well. Besides running book centers and helping to write, edit, and print books, they continued to visit people in their homes. Sometimes sisters would stay on the road for days or weeks, living with families in whatever parishes they were visiting. They walked mile after mile. Between towns or parishes they accepted rides (for now automobiles were more common) or took the train.

"Have you heard the news?"

It was a summer evening in 1936. One of the sisters in Alba was eager to share the latest news with two sisters returning from a trip.

"Not yet, Sister. What happened?"

"The Founder has moved to Rome! Father Timothy will be coming back to Alba to take charge of the Society here."

Father James had been thinking about moving to Rome for quite a while. Every international congregation had its headquarters there, at the center of the Catholic Church. Because the Founder intended his congregations to be international, Rome was the right place for him to be.

By this time, the Pauline congregations already owned a large piece of land in Rome. Facing one street was a building in which the Society of Saint Paul lived and worked. The sisters lived and worked in a building facing a different street, at the other end of the property. Father James hoped to build a large church between the two buildings once they had enough money to start.

The Founder enjoyed being in Rome. Before long, he began teaching the Pauline seminarians and directing the production of Bibles and books.

One day, after Sister Tecla had also moved to Rome, the Founder told her, "When I was at Saint Bernard's in Narzole back in 1908, I thought it would be good if there were a congregation of sisters to help priests in parish work."

As Sister Tecla listened with interest, Father James continued, "Their purpose would be to teach religion to children of all ages, visit the sick, comfort people preparing for death, and help priests in other ways."

"I like the idea," Sister Tecla replied.

"We are ready to launch that congregation now," James continued. "Some young Daughters of Saint Paul can be the first members."

Plans were made, and on October 7, 1938, the Sisters of Jesus the Good Shepherd (Pastoral Sisters) were founded. With the help of generous friends, Father James bought them a country house south of Rome. He visited the young sisters often and taught them the special way they would serve the Church.

By now, Father James had begun calling his various congregations "the Pauline Family." Though each had its own role in the Church, he wanted the congregations to help one another, like members of a family.

One evening, while most of the priests in the Rome community were relaxing in their living room, the Founder walked in. Father James looked around to be sure that many of them were present. He had been waiting for an opportunity to tell them something important. He had read an article about a missionary in Africa, whose life story would make a good film, and he had already spoken to several of the priests about it. Now he cleared his throat and waited until everyone was quiet.

"Regarding that film," he said, "we're going to make it. We've postponed making movies long enough. If Saint Paul were here today, he would already have made *several* films! He spread the message of Jesus in every way he could. And that's what we're going to do too."

The Founder looked around again. Seeing that some of the priests looked happy while others appeared worried, he continued, "God will be with us. Don't worry about money."

The work began. One of the Pauline priests directed the film. Priests from two other religious congregations helped write the script and prepare the film in other ways. Actors were hired. The filming was

"If Saint Paul were here today, he would already have made several films!"

done in Italy and in Africa. And when the movie came out, it won an award!

More importantly, it was a beginning. More films quickly followed. But World War II would delay many of the Founder's projects.

21

TO THE ENDS OF THE EARTH

On an evening in 1940, air raid sirens shrieked, warning of a possible attack. The house of the Society of Saint Paul in Rome quickly became dark. It was a blackout, meaning that the lights had been turned off so the house would not be a target for bombs. Men and boys felt their way down the staircase in the dark and gathered in the basement to wait for what might happen next. Many of them were afraid.

Father James followed them part of the way. Then he stopped at the top of the basement stairs. The priests and young people could see him outlined against a first-floor window. From time to time, he moved, and they saw that he was holding a rosary. During the whole air raid alert, he stayed there—sometimes standing still, sometimes pacing back and forth—praying.

The Founder was praying for all his spiritual children. Throughout his life, in times of greatest need, he had always turned to Mary. Now he did so again. *Mary,*

Queen of the Apostles, he prayed, *I beg you to ask God to protect all the Pauline priests, brothers, and sisters in Europe and Asia. Wherever the war is, I ask you to watch over your sons and daughters.*

He had long wanted to build a church in honor of Mary. Now he promised Jesus and Mary that if all the Paulines came through the war safely, he would build Mary's church in thanksgiving.

Some members of the Pauline Family suffered very much during the war. Many Paulines in Europe lived through air raids one night after another. A number of them had little to eat for months, even years. Some members of the Society of Saint Paul spent the war in a concentration camp in India. But not a single member of the Pauline Family was killed during the war.

In 1945, when the war was over, Father James began to plan the building of the church in honor of the Queen of the Apostles in Rome. He was also eager to send out priests, brothers, and sisters to nations all over the world. He wanted new houses of the Pauline Family everywhere, so that people everywhere in the world could know about Jesus. Later he would travel to visit his sons and daughters all over the world.

In June, 1946, Father James received an urgent phone call from Alba. Father Francis was very ill. The Founder hurried from Rome to the bedside of his friend. Father Francis's face lit up when he came into the room. "I'm so glad you've come," said Father Francis. "Please hear my confession."

"I will, and then you hear mine."

After each had received the Sacrament of Reconciliation, Father James said, "I owe you so much. Thank you for all you've done to help the foundation and growth of the Pauline Family."

His friend smiled. "I've always been a Pauline at heart and never regretted it."

A few days later, Father Francis passed away.

That same year, Father Timothy came back to Rome. He returned from Alba because the Founder needed his help. Father James asked him to obtain the Vatican's approval for the Disciples of the Divine

Master as a separate congregation. Father Timothy worked on the project together with a priest and a bishop from the Vatican. As the months went by, Father Timothy became weak and tired. A doctor tried to treat him, but nothing seemed to help.

On January 12, 1948, Pope Pius XII signed the document of approval for the Disciples of the Divine Master. That same day, after celebrating Mass, Father Timothy returned to his room in great pain. A new doctor was called in, who discovered something the previous doctor had not understood: The good priest had leukemia and was near death. Father Timothy lasted only twelve days after that diagnosis. At his bedside, saying good-bye, Father James told him, "You've always been my good and faithful son." The Founder could hardly hold back his tears.

Father Francis had been like a father to the Founder, and Father Timothy had been like a son. Now, Father James had lost them both. Yet, he hadn't lost his eagerness to carry out the mission God had given him. He prayed many hours each day and felt the Lord telling him to do more and more—not by himself, of course, but through the work of Paulines all over the world. The Society of Saint Paul began radio broadcasting, first in Italy, then in Japan. Other nations would follow. Later, the Daughters of Saint Paul, too, would reach out with radio. The Disciples of the Divine Master and the Pastoral Sisters were also working hard to make Christ better known.

Many people in Europe were discouraged after the destruction caused by five and a half years of war. "We can help them with films that show good values and give them hope," the Founder said. The Daughters of Saint Paul began to collect uplifting movies and rent them out to parishes. Soon, the Society began producing its own movies again. The whole Pauline Family worked together to help people all over the world learn about Jesus, the Divine Master and Good Shepherd, the Way, the Truth, and the Life.

By now the Founder's hair was no longer black but white. He looked even smaller and weaker than ever, and he wore thick glasses. But his eyes continued to shine. There was still something about him that made people listen to him and want to do what he asked. They could tell that he was doing what God wanted him to do.

One of the people he impressed was John Ferrero (Fay-RAY-roh), a businessman who lived in northern Italy. He had loaned the Founder some money and sent his partner to Rome to collect the repayment. The partner returned without the money.

"What happened?" asked Mr. Ferrero.

"He didn't hand it over," replied the partner. "He said he'll come to see you soon."

"You don't know how to take care of these things," said Mr. Ferrero.

Soon afterward, Father James went to visit Mr. Ferrero.

"How did it go?" the partner asked later. "Did he return the money?"

"No," said Mr. Ferrero, turning red. "I gave him more."

John Ferrero may have been one of the thousands of people who helped pay for the church of Mary, Queen of the Apostles, which now stands in Rome between the houses of the Society of Saint Paul and the Daughters of Saint Paul. The Founder had kept his wartime promise.

22

It Was the Right Road

By the 1950s there were Pauline communities all over the world. The Founder was busier than ever. He made several trips by air to Asia, Australia, and the Americas—sometimes alone, sometimes with Sister Tecla.

The Society of Saint Paul was producing more films. The Daughters of Saint Paul designed and made the costumes. A series of short films about the sacraments and commandments helped people grow in their faith. Full-length films about events from the Bible made the Word of God come alive for everyone. Movies, magazines, and music recordings were some of the ways Paulines nourished the faith of people everywhere. Everyone in the Pauline Family was dedicated to helping people deepen their relationship with God.

Meanwhile, new groups called secular institutes were starting up in the Church. People who joined these groups lived in their own homes and held regular jobs. By the good lives they lived, they showed other people how to be real followers of Jesus. Father James liked the idea of secular institutes. He started one for single men that he called the Institute of Saint Gabriel the Archangel, another for single women called the Institute of Mary of the Annunciation, and a third for diocesan priests and bishops called the Institute of Jesus the Priest.

Around the same time, Father James founded his fourth congregation of sisters. They were called the Sisters of Mary, Queen of Apostles. The members of this congregation helped young men and women discover God's plan for their lives. The Pauline Family was growing again.

Pope John XXIII wanted the Church to keep up with the changing times. He called the bishops of the world to meet at the Vatican. This great event was called the Second Vatican Council. For four years, from 1962 to 1965, the bishops met for several weeks every autumn in Saint Peter's Basilica, the huge church at the Vatican. More than two thousand, five hundred bishops attended! The superiors of some international religious congregations also attended. Father James was one of them.

Every day that the council met, the Founder went to Saint Peter's to listen to the discussions. When the four years were over, he told his Paulines, "We're on the right road. The bishops agree that it's important to use films, radio, and television to tell people about Jesus. They emphasize the importance of the Eucharist and the Bible. They agree that we must bring the Good News of Jesus to everyone. We've believed all this since we started." The Founder had been ahead of his times; God had shown him the way.

During those years of the Second Vatican Council, Sister Tecla suffered a stroke and lost her ability to speak. The Daughters of Saint Paul brought her to the hospital, where she stayed for several months, until she passed away.

"You'll have other superiors," the Founder told the Daughters of Saint Paul, "but you won't have another mother." In fact, Sister Tecla Merlo had been like a mother to many members of the Pauline congregations. Most of them remember her as Mother Tecla.

Father James was still on fire to do as much as possible for God and the Church. He thought back to those early days when he hadn't been sure what God wanted him to do. *Even then,* he thought, *I knew I wouldn't be working alone. I'd be working with other people. Now, those "other people" belong to five religious congregations, the Pauline Cooperators, and three secular institutes. They live and work all over the world. Yet, how much more good there is to do!*

In addition to publishing books and magazines, Paulines began using the radio more. In Italy and Brazil, Pauline congregations were producing phonograph records. In the newly independent African nations, Paulines were using colorful posters to teach religion. Father James was interested in all these new ways of making God better known and loved.

In June, 1969, hundreds of members of the Pauline Family gathered at the Vatican. Their Founder was going to receive a special award from Pope Paul VI. It was called "For the Church and the Pope."

Father James accepted the honor quietly. *It's not for me,* he thought. *I only tried to do what the Lord wanted. I'm accepting it for all these dear members of the Pauline Family who have followed me.*

Finally, at eighty-five, the Founder was slowing down. In August of that same year Father Louis Zanoni (Zuh-NOH-nee) took Father James's place as superior of the Society of Saint Paul. Father Louis asked the priests to start another secular institute that Father James wanted. This one would be for married couples. The Holy Family Institute would make the Pauline Family complete.

Now that he had more time, Father James spent each day praying. He had always prayed several Rosaries every day, and now he prayed still more.

Two faithful helpers made sure he had everything he needed. They were Brother Silvano (Seel-VAH-noh) of the Society of Saint Paul and Sister Judith of the Disciples of the Divine Master.

When people came to say hello to the Founder and asked what they could do for him, he would say, "Pray, pray." Sometimes his eyes would fill with tears. It was hard for him to say much, and difficult for him to remember people.

Toward the end of November, 1971, Father James became more seriously ill, and Pope Paul VI came to pray at his bedside.

Later that same day Father James told the spiritual sons and daughters who surrounded him, "I'm dying." Then he exclaimed, "Heaven!" Later he added, "I'm praying for everyone."

Those were his last words. Father James Alberione passed away on the afternoon of November 26 at the age of eighty-seven.

Thirty-one years later, on April 27, 2003, members from every branch of the Pauline family from every corner of the world gathered at Saint Peter's Basilica in Rome to witness the beatification of Father James Alberione. During the Mass Pope John Paul II told all of Blessed James's spiritual sons and daughters to be faithful to their Founder's example of great trust and zeal for God's plan of bringing the Gospel to all people in every way possible. Today the Pauline Family continues to follow in Blessed James's footsteps and bring the news of Jesus to the world. Blessed James's spiritual sons and daughters use books, radio, movies, computers, the Internet, music, sculptures, all forms of liturgical art, and anything else that may be invented to help people of all times and places to know God.

Blessed James Alberione, pray for us, that we too may be filled with a desire to tell others about God and his love for all people.

Prayer

Blessed James, like St. Paul, you had one Love—Jesus Christ—and one burning desire: to bring him to everyone. Help me to love the Lord Jesus as you loved him. Teach me how to show my love for him by the way I live. I do not yet know what my vocation in life will be, but pray for me, that I may be open to using my gifts so that others may know Jesus better. Help me to always trust God and his plan for me. I look forward to someday meeting you and all the saints in the joy of the Blessed Trinity. Amen.

Glossary

1. Adoration—worship; the greatest honor, given only to God. Eucharistic Adoration is a time of prayer before Jesus in the Holy Eucharist.

2. Bookbinding—fastening a book together and attaching a cover to it.

3. Bishop—a priest who has been ordained as a successor of the apostles. The leader of a diocese is a bishop; he may have other bishops as helpers.

4. Blessed Sacrament—another name for the Holy Eucharist, the real Body and Blood of the risen Jesus present under the appearances of bread and wine.

5. Cassock—an ankle-length robe sometimes worn by priests and seminarians.

6. Cathedral—the main church in a diocese.

7. Diocese—a part of the Church made up of Catholics within a certain geographical area.

8. **Founder**—a person who starts a new organization, such as a religious congregation.

9. **Meditation**—a form of mental prayer in which a person thinks about God in order to grow closer to him.

10. **Missionary**—a person who tells others about Jesus, often traveling to distant places to do so.

11. **Ordain**—to give the sacrament of Holy Orders, which makes a man either a deacon, a priest, or a bishop. Bishops are the ones who ordain.

12. **Pact**—an agreement in which two or more persons make promises to one another.

13. **Patron saint**—a special saint who protects and prays for a particular person or for a particular group, such as a religious congregation.

14. **Profession, religious**—a ceremony in which a man becomes a religious priest or brother or a woman becomes a religious sister.

15. **Rector**—the priest in charge of a seminary.

16. Rectory—the house where the pastor of a parish and other parish priests live.

17. Religious congregation—a group of men or women who have taken religious vows and usually live together in one or more communities.

18. Seminarian—a man who is preparing to become a priest.

19. Superior—the person in charge of a religious community or congregation.

20. Tabernacle—a container in a church or chapel where the Holy Eucharist is kept.

21. Vatican—the small, independent country where the Pope lives; also, the governing organization of the Church, with the Pope as its head.

22. Vocation—a call from God to a certain way of life. A person may have a vocation to the married life, the priesthood, the religious life, or the single life. Everyone has a vocation to be holy.

23. Vow—an important promise freely made to God.

The Daughters of St. Paul operate book and media centers at the following addresses. Visit, call, or write the one nearest you today, or find us at www.pauline.org.

CALIFORNIA	
3908 Sepulveda Blvd, Culver City, CA 90230	310-397-8676
935 Brewster Ave., Redwood City, CA 94063	650-369-4230
5945 Balboa Avenue, San Diego, CA 92111	858-565-9181
FLORIDA	
145 S.W. 107th Avenue, Miami, FL 33174	305-559-6715
HAWAII	
1143 Bishop Street, Honolulu, HI 96813	808-521-2731
Neighbor Islands call:	866-521-2731
ILLINOIS	
172 North Michigan Avenue, Chicago, IL 60601	312-346-4228
LOUISIANA	
4403 Veterans Memorial Blvd, Metairie, LA 70006	504-887-7631
MASSACHUSETTS	
885 Providence Hwy, Dedham, MA 02026	781-326-5385
MISSOURI	
9804 Watson Road, St. Louis, MO 63126	314-965-3512
NEW YORK	
64 West 38th Street, New York, NY 10018	212-754-1110
PENNSYLVANIA	
Philadelphia—relocating	215-676-9494
SOUTH CAROLINA	
243 King Street, Charleston, SC 29401	843-577-0175
VIRGINIA	
1025 King Street, Alexandria, VA 22314	703-549-3806
CANADA	
3022 Dufferin Street, Toronto, ON M6B 3T5	416-781-9131